Handwriting

Book 6

Sue Peet

William Collins' dream of knowledge for all began with the publication of his first book in 1819. A self-educated mill worker, he not only enriched millions of lives, but also founded a flourishing publishing house. Today, staying true to this spirit, Collins books are packed with inspiration, innovation and practical expertise. They place you at the centre of a world of possibility and give you exactly what you need to explore it.

Collins. Freedom to teach.

Published by Collins
An imprint of HarperCollinsPublishers
77–85 Fulham Palace Road
Hammersmith
London
W6 8JB

Browse the complete Collins
Education catalogue at
www.collinseducation.com

Text, design and illustrations © HarperCollins*Publishers* Ltd 2011

Previously published as *Spectrum Handwriting* by Folens Ltd,
first published 2000.

10 9 8 7 6 5 4 3
ISBN: 978-0-00-742707-9

British Library Cataloguing in Publication Data
A Catalogue record for this publication is available from the British Library.

Acknowledgements
Fonts from *Handwriting for Windows* used with the permission of KBER.
Extract from 'Beowulf', translated by Kevin Crossley-Holland and Charles Keeping
(Oxford University Press).
Extract from 'Street Child' by Berlie Doherty.
Extract from 'The Dark is Rising' by Susan Cooper.

The author and publisher wish to thank the following for permission to use copyright material: United Agents Limited for the poem 'Gruesome' by Roger McGough from You Tell Me, copyright © Roger McGough 1979. Reproduced by permission of United Agents (www.unitedagents.co.uk) on behalf of Roger McGough; The poems 'Believing' and 'Celebration' from Spooky Rhymes by Willis Hall. Reproduced by permission of the Agency (London) Ltd, copyright © Willis Hall. All rights reserved and enquiries to the The Agency (London) ltd, 24 Pottery Lane, London W11 4LZ info@theagency.co.uk. Quotations by Sir Winston Churchill between 20th August 1940 and 26th June 1954, copyright © Winston S. Churchill. Reproduced with permission of Curtis Brown Ltd London on behalf of The Estate of Sir Winston Churchill; and the poem "Picking Teams" from Please Mrs Butler by Allan Ahlberg, (Kestrel, 1983, Puffin Books, 1984), copyright © Allan Ahlberg, 1983.

Every effort has been made to trace copyright holders and to obtain their permission for the use of copyright material. The author and publisher will gladly receive any information enabling them to rectify any error or omission in subsequent editions.

Design: Mark Walker
Illustrations: Chantal Kees
Cover design: LCD
Cover illustration: Gwyneth Williamson

Printed by RR Donnelley at Glasgow, UK.

To install the pre-cursive and cursive
fonts used in this series, please visit
www.kber.co.uk, and purchase a licence for
Handwriting for Windows Version 3.0.

Contents

Programme overview

Book	Age	Main Content	Main Teaching Aims	Primary National Strategy	Cambridge International Primary Programme
A	Age 4–5 Nursery/Reception/P1 Foundation stage	Pencil control Hand-eye coordination Movements necessary to form letters	To make controlled pencil movements To join two points with a straight or curved line To follow a given sequence of movements	Use a pencil and hold it effectively to form recognisable letters, most of which are correctly formed	
B	Age 4–5 Reception/P1	Pencil control Letter-like movements Recognition of lower case letters linked to upper case letters Upper case letters (alphabetical order) Numbers 0–9	To produce a comfortable pencil grip To produce a controlled line that supports letter formation To write upper case letters using the correct sequence of movements To recognise lower case letters	Use a pencil and hold it effectively to form recognisable letters, most of which are correctly formed	
1A	Age 5–6 Year 1/P2 (Term 1)	Precursive lower case letters, grouped according to movement Recognition of lower case joins Upper and lower case links	To develop a comfortable and efficient pencil grip for forming and linking letters To recognise upper and lower case counterparts To form lower case letters correctly in a script that will be easy to join	Write most letters, correctly formed and orientated, using a comfortable and efficient pencil grip	Develop a comfortable and efficient pencil grip Form letters correctly
1B	Age 5–6 Year 1/P2 (Terms 2 and 3)	Lower case letter formation and joins in a cursive style using common rime patterns Main punctuation marks	To reinforce the link between handwriting, spelling and the recognition of phonic patterns and letter strings To practise correct letter orientation, formation and proportion	Write most letters, correctly formed and orientated, using a comfortable and efficient pencil grip Write with spaces between words accurately	Develop a comfortable and efficient pencil grip Form letters correctly
2	Age 6–7 Year 2/P3	High-frequency word practice Print in the environment Letter joins through common spelling patterns and strings Print for labels, notices etc. School and classroom vocabulary Beginnings of self-assessment	Practice in basic sight vocabulary Reinforcement and practice using the four basic handwriting diagonal and horizontal joins Linking handwriting to phonic and spelling knowledge and patterns Conceptual awareness of space required for printing (for labels, notices etc.)	Write legibly, using upper and lower case letters appropriately within words, and observing correct spacing within and between words Form and use the four basic handwriting joins	Form letters correctly and consistently Practise handwriting patterns and the joining of letters

Scottish Curriculum for Excellence
First stage, Writing (Tools for writing): I can present my writing in a way that will make it legible and attractive for my reader (LIT 1-24a)

National Curriculum for Wales
Foundation Stage objective: develop a legible style of handwriting in order to follow the conventions of written English and Welsh

Revised Northern Ireland Curriculum
Key Stage 1 objective: use a legible style of handwriting

Book	Age	Main Content	Main Teaching Aims	Primary National Strategy	Cambridge International Primary Programme
3	Age 7–8 Year 3/P4	Reinforcement and practice of print and cursive style Copy writing Uses to which handwriting may be put High-frequency word practice Development of spelling patterns	Reinforcement and practice of cursive and printed style to ensure consistency in size and proportion of letters and the spacing between letters and words Purposes and uses of handwriting and print	Write with consistency in the size and proportion of letters and spacing within and between words, using the correct formation of handwriting joins	Ensure consistency in the size and proportion of letters and the spacing of words Practise joining letters in handwriting Build up handwriting speed, fluency and legibility
4	Age 8–9 Year 4/P5	Copy writing Uses to which handwriting may be put High-frequency word practice Development of spelling patterns Development of a personal style Speed writing practice	Reinforcement and practice of cursive and printed style to ensure consistency in size and proportion of letters and the spacing between letters and words Purposes and uses of handwriting and print Consolidation and development of a style that is fast, fluent and legible Presentation, layout and decoration of 'finished' work	Write consistently with neat, legible and joined handwriting	Use joined-up handwriting in all writing
5	Age 9–10 Year 5/P6	Copy writing Development of a personal style Speed writing practice Uses to which handwriting may be put	Purposes and uses of handwriting and print Consolidation and development of a style that is fast, fluent and legible Presentation, layout and decoration of 'finished' work	Adapt handwriting for specific purposes, for example printing, use of italics	Review, revise and edit writing in order to improve it, using IT as appropriate
6	Age 10–11 Year 6/P7	Copy writing Development of a personal style Speed writing practice Uses to which handwriting may be put Links into ICT and fonts	Purposes and uses of handwriting and print Consolidation and development of a style that is fast, fluent and legible Presentation, layout and decoration of 'finished' work	Use different styles of handwriting for different purposes with a range of media, developing a consistent and personal legible style Select from a wide range of ICT programs to present text effectively and communicate information and ideas	Use different genres as models for writing Use IT effectively to prepare and present writing for publication

Scottish Curriculum for Excellence
Second stage, Writing (Tools for writing): I consider the impact that layout and presentation will have and can combine lettering, graphics and other features to engage my reader (LIT 2-24a)

National Curriculum for Wales
Key Stage 2 objective: present writing appropriately (develop legible handwriting; using appropriate features of layout and presentation, including ICT)

Revised Northern Ireland Curriculum
Key Stage 2 objective: develop a swift and legible style of handwriting

Teacher notes

General introduction

Collins Primary Focus: Handwriting is a comprehensive programme designed to support teachers and children through the stages of learning a clear, fluent, legible and fast style of joined writing from the early stages to the top of the Primary phase. The programme provides copiable material that is intended for use through shared sessions, guided group tuition and individual practice.

The programme begins with patterns and movements, which will be necessary to improve hand-eye coordination, fine motor control and individual letter production.

Linked to National Curriculum levels and the Primary National Strategy, the programme encourages a precursive and then a cursive style from the early stages of learning.

The programme aims to link the development of handwriting skills and style to the main patterns and rules of the English spelling system. As children practise the movements necessary to make the joins and patterns of the handwriting scheme, they are also reinforcing the patterns of the main onset, rime and spelling patterns.

By Book 2, children are provided with an opportunity to experiment with alternative letter shapes when forming their own personal handwriting style.

Books 3–6 introduce the notion of keeping a Handwriting folder containing samples of material that will prove useful when presenting and setting out work for publication. The books include many uses to which both printing and joined handwriting skills may be put.

Books 3–6 also introduce the concept of two types of handwriting: one style may be used for 'speed' tasks, e.g. personal note-taking; the other, neater, style may be used for presentational work. Self-assessment sheets are included in Book 3 (pp.20 and 63) and Book 6 (p.20). Books 3–6 also link handwriting skills to the basic skills of layout and presentation on a computer keyboard.

The joining of letters in words: which style is most appropriate?

Teachers will always have views about the efficacy or attractiveness of specific letterforms.

It must be remembered that every adult will consider the formation that they use to be the most comfortable to them. However, this does not necessarily make it the most effective formation for children learning for the first time. Teachers must bear in mind the need to develop a handwriting style that is clear, fluent, legible and fast for children learning for the first time.

What about exceptions?

For children with dyspraxia or other handwriting difficulties, the teacher may need to look for SEN support. These children may already be receiving handwriting tuition as part of their support.

Children who move schools may well have already learned another handwriting style. If they enter school during the Infant stage, teachers may wish them to recap pages from the previous book, and this may be completed – with the cooperation of parents – as a homework activity. Children who move schools during the Junior stage may well have formed a personal handwriting style, which, although different, is clear, fluent and legible. It may be inappropriate to alter their handwriting style at this stage.

The notes on particular handwriting difficulties (see p.14 of the Teacher notes in Books 1A–2) may also provide useful information.

Letterforms in the programme

Collins Primary Focus: Handwriting aims for the development of joined handwriting as soon as individual precursive letterforms have been mastered. Specific letterforms have been selected to meet the following criteria:

- They should help children's handwriting to be clear, fluent, legible and fast.
- Each individual lower case letter chosen begins from the main writing line.
- Each lower case letter is taught with both a lead-in and a lead-out stroke. This is to help avoid confusion in young children about whether to

begin a letter at the top or the bottom. It has also proved to be beneficial for children with poor hand control and for dyslexic children.

- The joined lower case letters should, where possible, resemble closely their printed counterparts.
- Letters, such as 's' should have the same form wherever they occur in a word, thus reducing the amount that children need to relearn.
- It is possible to join all lower case letters. One letter ('f') changes from the precursive to the cursive stage. While it is felt that the 'f' used in Book B will be familiar to young children learning to form the precursive letters, the cursive 'f' is used from Book 1A to encourage a more fluent hand.
- The pencil or pen should need to be lifted from the page as little as possible when linking lower case letters in words, thus reinforcing the patterning of joined movements within letter strings as an aid to memorising phonic and spelling patterns.

Precursive Upright (Book B)

A B C D E F G H I J K L M
N O P Q R S T U V W X Y Z
a b c d e f g h i j k l m
n o p q r s t u v w x y z
The quick brown fox jumps over the lazy dog.

Cursive Upright (Books 1A–1B)

A B C D E F G H I J K L M
N O P Q R S T U V W X Y Z
a b c d e f g h i j k l m
n o p q r s t u v w x y z
The quick brown fox jumps over the lazy dog.

Cursive Slanted (Books 2–6)

A B C D E F G H I J K L M
N O P Q R S T U V W X Y Z
a b c d e f g h i j k l m
n o p q r s t u v w x y z
The quick brown fox jumps over the lazy dog.

The following letter styles have been chosen to meet the preceding list of criteria:

Specific letter style options

The reasoning behind each cursive letter style option chosen for use in *Collins Primary Focus: Handwriting* was discussed with several Literacy and SpLD (Dyslexic) practitioners who agreed with the choices.

f	Chosen because, looped from the back, it is easiest to link to all other letters, always joining the same way and thus more fluent.
s	Chosen because it joins in the same way whether it is at the beginning, in the middle or at the end of a word, thus making it fluent and meaning there is less for children to learn.
v	Chosen because it is more legible, most like the printed 'v' and less likely to be confused with the letter 'u'.
w	Chosen because it is more legible, most like the printed 'w' and less likely to be confused with the letter 'u'.
x	This is the only small letter that requires the pencil/pen to be lifted from the paper. This style was chosen because it will join and because it is most like its precursive counterpart. A curved 'x' can often be confused for the letters 'sc'; this is particularly so for dyslexic and less able readers.
y	Chosen because it is more legible, most like the printed 'y' and doesn't involve taking the pencil/pen off the paper.
z	Chosen because it will join and because it is most like its precursive counterpart.

As children move on to join letters in words, they will learn that many letters will join in different places, depending on the letter they are linked to. The programme aims to support the development of strong links between the formation of patterns in handwriting and those involved in phonic and spelling knowledge.

Contents of the programme

Infant Stage

Book A: Foundation Stage and Reception/P1

This book introduces the fine motor movements and pencil control that will be necessary for the formation of letters and patterns. It provides practice in moving from left to right, keeping within 'tramlines' and making the up-and-down and curved movements necessary for letter formation.

Book B: Reception/P1

This book reinforces movements and patterns that will help children to make the movements they will need when learning to form letter shapes. For many children the movements from left to right and from top to bottom may not be intuitive, hence the instruction to 'Start at the ☆.'

Practice is also provided in each of the movements for upper case letters. These have been placed early in the programme because many children will have learned at least some of these letters before they begin formal schooling, and so any inappropriate movements can be corrected early.

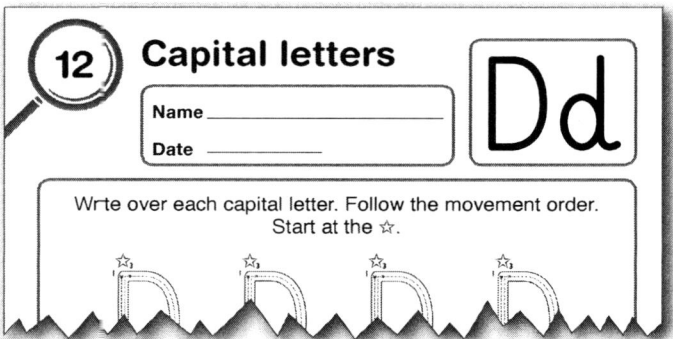

Book 1A: Year 1/P2 (Term 1)

Linked closely to the National Curriculum and Primary National Strategy, this book provides more intense teaching strategies and practice for the first term of formal tuition.

Since it is at this stage that children may learn incorrect or inappropriate movements, each individual letter shape and movement is taught with a lead-in and a lead-out stroke beginning from the writing line. The letters are grouped according to the main movements involved so that children gain extra reinforcement of the shapes and movements involved. By grouping letters according to their movement, it is also hoped to avoid the confusion that many children encounter between letters that may look very similar in print, e.g. 'b' and 'd', 'p' and 'q', 'n' and 'h'.

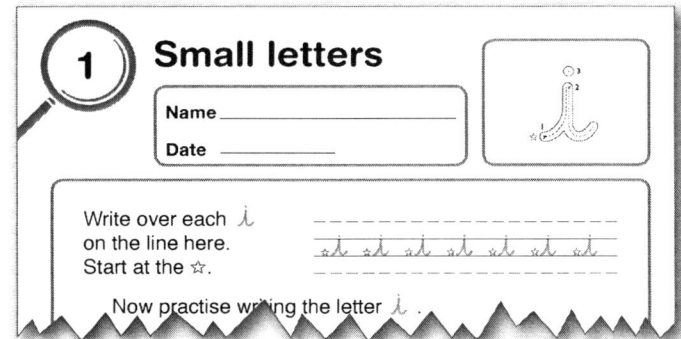

Book 1B: Year 1/P2 (Terms 2 and 3)

To provide extra practice in the transition from precursive to cursive letters, an extra book has been included at this stage. In this book, upper case letters and lower case letters are reinforced through some of the main rime patterns that will be used for spelling. In this way the development of a cursive hand is linked to the introduction of spelling patterns.

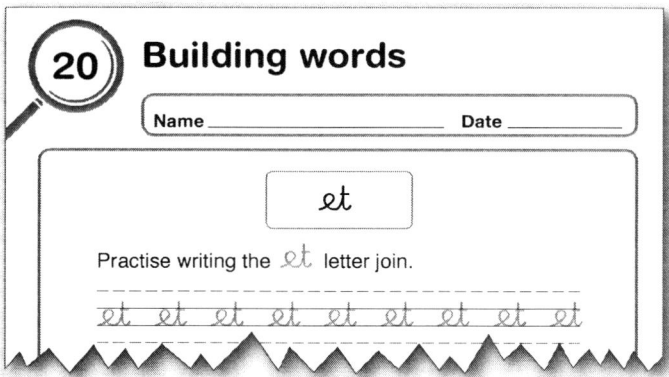

Book 2: Year 2/P3

This book continues the development of linking handwriting to spelling, introducing joins through the main onset groups and blends and the high-frequency words required to be learned and practised by the end of the Infant stage.

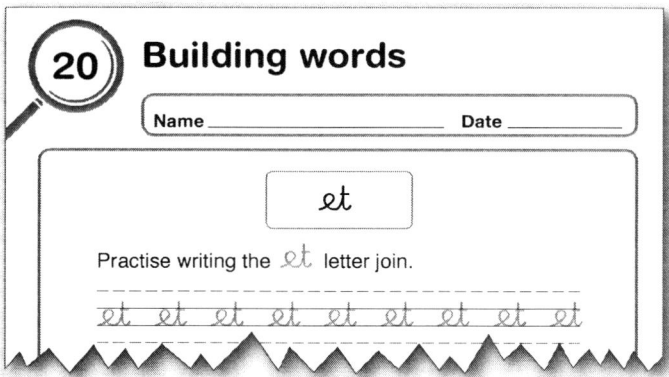

Junior Stage

Book 3: Year 3/P4

This book reinforces the handwriting style already learned, through sentences, spelling patterns and simple tongue-twisters and rhymes. During this book, children are encouraged to attempt writing with their eyes closed to help fix the pattern of movements in the mind. (It may be helpful if teachers show children how to place their pencil or pen on the writing line before closing their eyes!)

Through this book, children are introduced to the idea of collating a Handwriting folder. Some tasks will need to be completed on another sheet of paper. This book also contains ideas for exemplar material to be retained by children in their Handwriting folder.

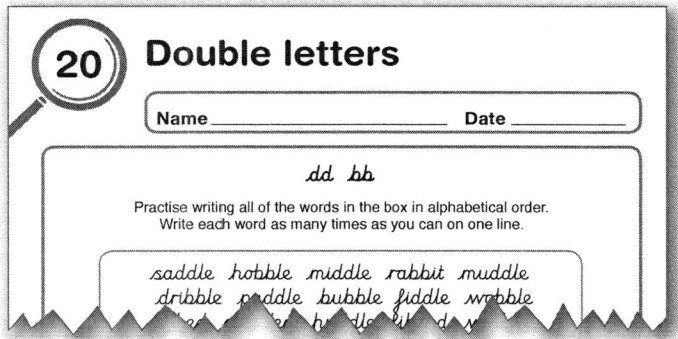

Book 4: Year 4/P5

At this stage, children are encouraged to examine different handwriting purposes and styles. This book also includes settings in which print letters may be appropriate both in upper case and lower case forms.

Links with common spelling rules and patterns and common high and medium-frequency vocabulary are continued. This book also introduces practice in writing at speed.

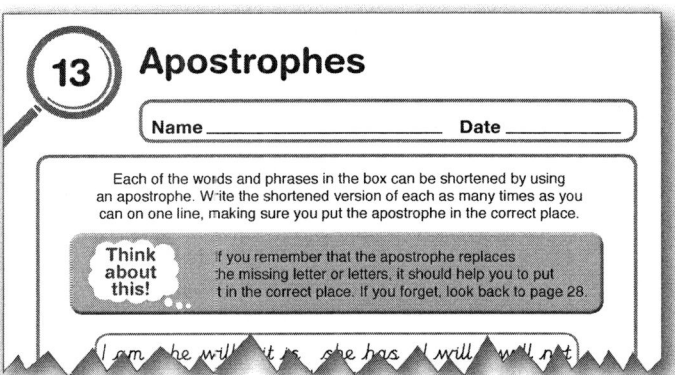

Book 5: Year 5/P6

Throughout this book, children explore different contexts in which a well-formed handwriting style plays an important part. They are asked to use both print and joined styles to transform material from a range of curricula and everyday situations for presentation to others. By this stage, children will be developing at least three handwriting styles (see pp.12–13).

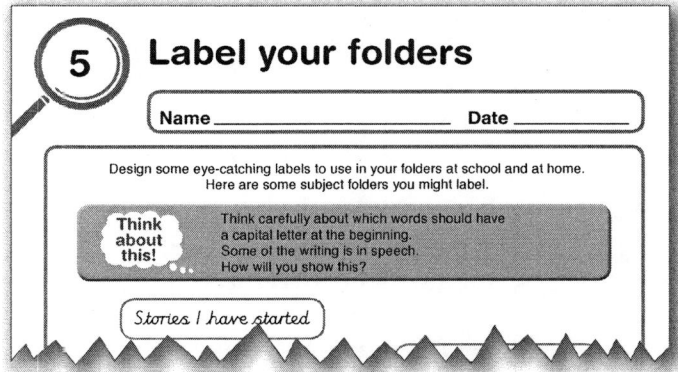

Book 6: Year 6/P7

This book extends children's mastery of the three forms of handwriting listed in the Book 5 entry on pp.12–13. Children are encouraged, through a variety of traditional calligraphy and modern presentational tasks, to develop a style that is personal and unique to themselves. (The relationship between hand-crafted and computer-aided design is extended.)

Points to remember when teaching handwriting

Seating

The seating of children for handwriting lessons is particularly important. For this reason, some teachers prefer to specify a 'handwriting table', where the light is particularly good and shines from the side or back of the children.

Many children find it more comfortable to slant their work to the side, away from their writing hand, so that they can clearly see what they are writing. For this reason, they may need more room for handwriting practice than may normally be available.

Left-handed children will need to be seated at the left-hand side of the table or desk. These children might also need a cushion or pad to provide extra height and may often benefit from a sloping surface, which might be provided by using a ring-binder file, on which to rest their paper.

Pencil/pen control

The pencil or pen should be gripped loosely between the first finger and thumb, using the second finger as a rest. The non-writing hand should be used to support and guide the paper. Many children do not learn this automatically, and it may need to be specifically taught.

Children may, even at a very early age, have learned an inappropriate grip. In some cases the hand may curl right over the pencil or pen, making their writing look extremely awkward. Teachers need to make several judgements before intervening to alter such a grip:

- If the child suffers from even a minor manual difficulty, the grip used may be the most comfortable to them.
- If their handwriting is clear, fluent, reasonably legible (to themselves and other children!) and reasonably fast, attempting to change their grip may do more harm than good. These children would benefit from the same practice in patterning and fluency as those with cramped or jerky hand movements. Tips on detecting and correcting difficulties can be found on pp.13–15 of the Teacher notes for Books 3 and 4.
- If altering the grip is the only solution, these children may benefit from recapping of earlier units in the programme as homework practice or in SEN support sessions, to help them relearn the correct movements.

Setting up a special handwriting table makes it easier to make pencil grips or triangular-shaped pencils or pens available for those children who find them more comfortable to use. Several suppliers make triangular-shaped pencils, which children may find more comfortable than a pencil grip.

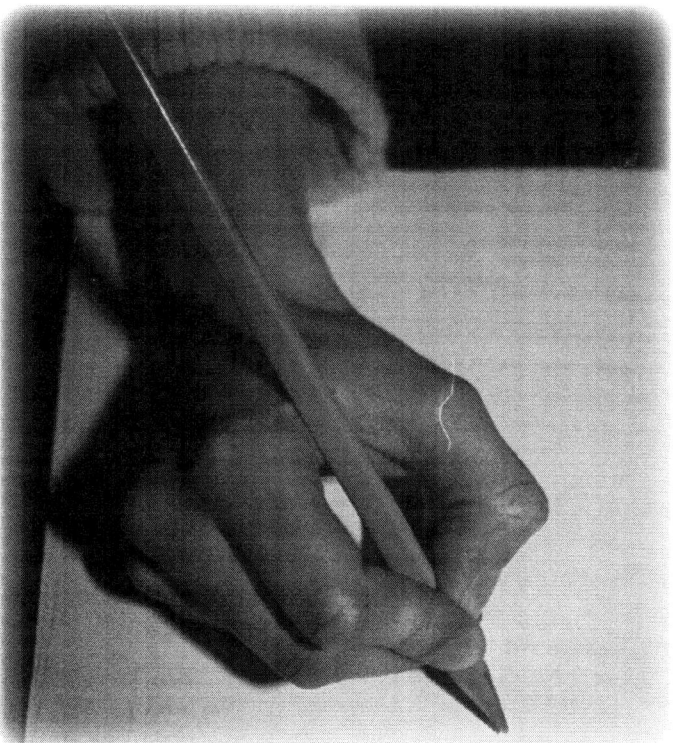

If the layout of the classroom precludes or hinders the setting-up of a handwriting table, children should be taught where their particular handwriting aids are kept and trained to find them for themselves before beginning their Handwriting lesson. Information about these implements and aids should also be made readily available to all staff members.

Materials and resources

School staff members, through their policy, may have personal preferences about whether pencil or pen should be used for 'best' handwriting. A range of implements and materials, however, should be made available to enable children to begin to make judgements and choices about what is most appropriate for a specific task. For example, children presenting shape poetry might choose to use 'jumbo' crayons or an italic pen to create a dramatic effect.

Some of the items that might be included in a resource box for handwriting are listed below.

Detailed notes on some of these resources may be found on pp.11–12 of the Teacher notes in Books 1A–2.

Pencils and pens

- A range of pencils of differing hardness. They should be of reasonable length and sharpened, but not to the point where they snap on use.
- Cartridge or fountain pens (because a pen, like a cook's knife, becomes shaped to a particular hand).
- Rollerball, felt-tip and fibre-tip pens.
- Coloured fibre-tip pens for artistic work.
- Italic pens (for all to try and for those who choose to create particular effects).

Paper

- Plenty of 'first draft' paper.
- Ruled guideline sheets for placing under work.
- Good-quality cartridge paper of different colours for 'best' presentation work. Teachers may wish to reserve this for special work.
- Different-sized paper, e.g. A4, A5, letter-size for notes and letters.
- Thin card, some of which might be pre-folded.
- Different-shaped papers and cards for poetry etc.
- Pre-decorated borders and mounts (preferably made in advance by the children).

Peripherals

- Triangular-shaped pencils and a selection of pencil grips.
- Ring-binder files or wedge-shaped blocks on which to rest and slant work.
- Rulers for measuring and to help keep lines straight.
- Cushions or seat pads to give extra height.

The writing environment

These items might be on display in the writing area:

- A sample sheet showing computer fonts available.
- Examples of computer-generated 'word art'.
- The alphabet in upper case and lower case letters.
- Exemplar material completed by children.
- Reminder notices, e.g. 'Don't forget the finger space!'

Organisation and timing of lessons

By this stage in the programme, many children will be gaining confidence in a joined handwriting style and may complete much of their work independent of direct support.

Some teachers will wish to continue the practice of a regular handwriting lesson (see p.13 of the Teacher notes in Books 1A-2). Even where teachers feel that they can integrate the teaching of handwriting with other aspects of Literacy, they will need to provide:

- Some opportunity within whole-class shared sessions, perhaps within the Literacy lesson, to demonstrate new points, emphasise the three different handwriting styles (see p.9), highlight class errors, or to link the purposes of handwriting to other work.
- Regular guided group sessions, preferably at least once a week/fortnight, in particular to observe specific children and to detect possible errors before they become entrenched.
- Support for children with specific handwriting difficulties.
- Daily opportunity for independent practice, possibly as homework.

NB: More detailed notes on the Handwriting lesson, Practice and reinforcement and Assessment may be found in the Teacher notes for Books 1A-2.

Handwriting and the use of ICT

It is now becoming possible to use a cursive font to demonstrate joined handwriting on computer. This may enable teachers to produce supplementary material for children to practise or examples of texts used for other aspects of the literacy lesson. Books 3–6 also suggest activities that may be completed using a computer keyboard. These are specifically intended to focus on layout, design and presentational skills.

Collins Primary Focus: Handwriting, in conjunction with handwriting computer software, aims to link manual handwriting with computer-generated handwriting from the earliest stages. Software may be used to create extra worksheets for practice and reinforcement. Children may also be able to print out their stories, poems and non-fiction writing using handwriting software that features a cursive style.

Book 5: Year 5/P6

Throughout this book, children explore different contexts in which a well-formed handwriting style plays an important part. They are asked to use both print and joined styles to transform material from a range of curricula and everyday situations for presentation to others. By this stage, children will be developing at least three handwriting styles:

- A neat, 'best' form for presentational work that may be produced slowly and with care. This style may be part of a 'school style'.
- A speedier and sometimes less neat form for, e.g. making personal notes or copying work to be presented later.

▼ 'Note' - writing done at speed.

If plants do not get enough light, they grow very tall and

▼ Too large spaces between words.

There are several different

▼ 'Best' handwriting.

The dog fetched the bone to the boy.

It is perfectly reasonable that some children using this style may begin to 'personalise' their writing. They may begin to add loops or serifs, adopt alternative letterforms and link upper case letters to lower case letters – as many adults do. They may also experiment with a unique signature at the foot of their work. This personalisation should be encouraged as long as it fits the criteria of being clear, fluent, legible and fast.

- A clear, well-formed print style for labels, notices, captions etc, demonstrating judgement about style, size, and spatial awareness of the room available.

Personalising a handwriting style

The focus of the handwriting lessons may now shift from the specific joins between lower case letters, towards issues of layout, design and presentation.

By Book 5 it will be entirely natural for children to begin to personalise their handwriting. Particularly within their personal 'note-making' hand, children may begin to opt for differences from the given style.

- Many children will automatically begin to join upper case letters at the beginning of sentences and words, to the lower case letters that follow. This is entirely natural and shows progression to an 'adult' style. Typewritten fonts do not yet have the capacity to do this and it will be for teachers (and perhaps the children themselves) to decide whether it is appropriate in the 'best' handwriting.
- Children may begin to adopt a stylish signature and this, again, should be encouraged provided that it is neat, fluent and legible!

- Some children will decide to adopt letter shapes other than those used in *Collins Primary Focus: Handwriting*. It should be remembered that the letter shapes selected were those that were considered to be most appropriate in order to teach a fluent, joined style for young children. It will be entirely in order for children who have mastered this, to substitute a 'pigeon' or rolling 's' for the letter selected for the screen; to alter their 'f' or 'w', or to add serifs and loops to upper case letters.
- The need for a fluent style, which can be produced at speed, will become paramount as children reach the top of Primary and move into Secondary school. The style of each letter in *Collins Primary Focus: Handwriting* was deliberately chosen with this in mind.

Teachers will need to decide whether to accept these differences within the material that is presented for display or publication. Inevitably, as children present material from a computer, they will opt for different fonts. Much may depend on whether the school has a policy of presenting material in a particular 'school style' (see p.14).

Many businesses have a 'house style' for all 'public' documentation that is linked to their corporate image and logo. The planning department of a whole city may choose a specific font and style to be used on all public buildings, vehicles and literature, to promote a positive image and reflect the ethos of the city. Activities within Books 5 and 6 encourage children to begin to make similar judgements about written material they present to others.

13

A school policy for handwriting

Whether a school has a <u>written</u> policy for handwriting or not, a policy will exist. Unfortunately, in the worst instances this policy varies from teacher to teacher and from class to class. Some schools have negotiated a 'school style' that their policy states will be used for all work for public display (see exceptions below). Whatever form the policy takes, certain factors need to be discussed by staff and taken into consideration.

When and how will handwriting be taught?

Handwriting has often been taught through separate lessons on a once or twice-weekly basis, and sometimes by a separate 'calligraphy' teacher. If a separate Handwriting teacher and lessons are adopted, it is important that all staff members remain closely aware of the content of these lessons so that practice and reinforcement may be continued in other lessons.

Collins Primary Focus: Handwriting has been designed to facilitate such an approach. Exemplar samples may be used for part of the shared session before children move on to guided groups. Group work may be the main vehicle of tuition, allowing teachers to focus on a small group of children at any one time. (Inappropriate habits may easily develop unnoticed in a whole-class lesson where the teacher cannot watch all children simultaneously.) Once teachers are sure that the group have understood any new strategies or skills, children may move on to reinforce and practise what they have learned in independent groups or individually. The guided group may also make it easier to identify the child or children that need extra or special teaching.

Practice and reinforcement

Ideally, children should have the opportunity to practise their handwriting skills for 10–15 minutes every day. Provided teachers have made sure that the teaching has been understood, this practice might be undertaken in independent activities both within the Literacy lesson and at other times during the school day. It might also be completed as homework.

Assessment

The principles of good handwriting are that it should be legible, fluent and comfortable to produce at speed. Some children will never be able to achieve the degree of neatness and consistency of others in the class.

Children should be encouraged to pay particular attention to handwriting when work is to be presented to others and at the publication stage of a piece of work. *Collins Primary Focus: Handwriting* encourages children from the start to make a self-assessment of their work, practising and reinforcing when necessary. At the foot of most of the resource sheets is a simple box to allow children to make a self-assessment of their work. Where children regularly work with a partner, they may be consulted before the boxes are completed. Self-assessment checklists are included in Book 3 (pp.20 and 63) and Book 6 (p.20).

Book 6

Year 6/P7 – Presentational writing

Using their own personal handwriting style, children will use extracts from literature, political speeches, poetry and famous quotations to produce exemplar material for presentation or display. Book 6 extends the notion of the different uses to which handwriting may be put and the presentational skills involved.

Page 17: Your Handwriting folder

Encourage children to be as innovative and individual as they can in making a cover for the folder that they will use to store their handwriting examples. They may choose to set their headings in a printed or joined style. They might decorate upper case letters and use patterns to decorate a border. Children who feel comfortable with desktop publishing tools may choose this medium to design and print their cover; or the activity might be set as homework.

Encourage children to include material drawn from outside the confines of the pages of the book, e.g. samples of handwritten or computer-generated 'word art'. They might also include samples of handwriting from different periods of history, or patterns that they wish to copy. They should be encouraged to take note of how handwriting, signwriting and presentational skills are used in the world around them, e.g. in shops, on TV and the internet, in film.

Page 18: Decorative patterns

Children should be encouraged to seek out patterns used in the world around them and examine how these are made. Often a seemingly complicated pattern is in fact made up of simply repeated straight lines and curves. Children may collect examples of these to use when decorating presented work in the classroom.

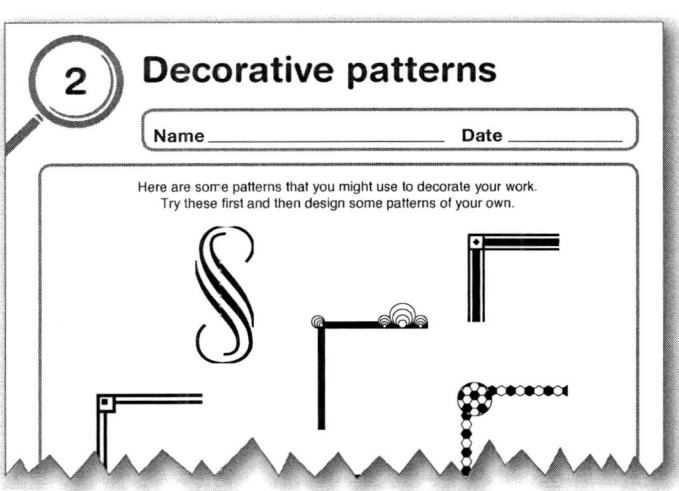

Page 20: My handwriting: a checklist

This checklist is designed to help children make their own assessment of how their handwriting performs in differing situations.

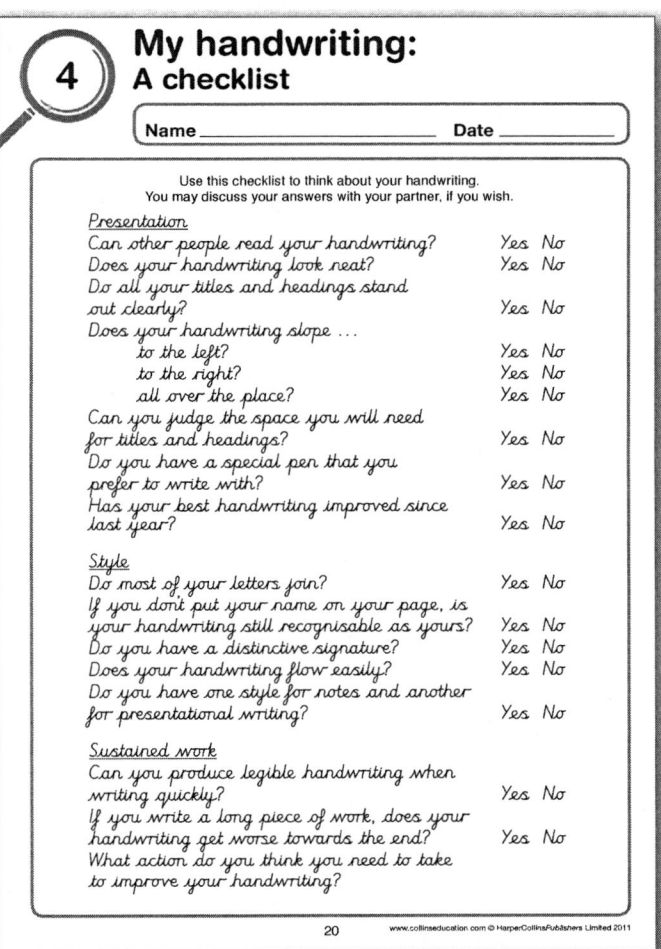

Page 21: All about me!

One of the most common problems with handwriting is its tendency to deteriorate towards the end of a sustained piece of work. While this may be unavoidable in rough work, children at the top of Primary school are preparing for the large bulk of writing they will be expected to undertake as they move into Secondary school. A pause in writing, even at speed, and a chance to relax the hand and shake and uncramp fingers, can ensure that the end of a sustained piece of writing remains legible.

Page 22: Text on a web page

Although many people feel that new technology will diminish the need for handwriting, the principles of spatial awareness, presentation and thought for the reader still apply. Many early web pages were felt to be overcrowded and poorly set out. Users of the internet found them confusing or too 'busy'. Since many children of this age will be working with ICT, they should be encouraged to make constructive criticism of what they see and suggest improvements to presentation and layout.

Pages 23–35

These pages provide examples of situations where handwriting and its presentation should be made to look as attractive as possible. Each activity requires a degree of spatial awareness of how much space letters and characters will take up and how they will look when set. Some pages are related to excerpts from literature. The aim should be for children to reproduce, in their own handwriting, favourite extracts from books or poems they have enjoyed. (Page 34 suggests some subtitles that might be used for an anthology of such extracts.)

13 **Handwriting check 2:**
"Gruesome"

Name _____ Date _____

Write this poem in your best handwriting and store it in your Handwriting folder. You might like to keep some more poems ready in case you need them.

...was sitting in the sitting room
toying with some toys
when from a door marked: "Gruesome"
There came a GRUESOME noise.

Cautiously I opened it
and there to my surprise
a little GRUE lay sitting
with tears in its eyes.

"Oh little GRUE please tell me
what is it ails you so?"
"Well I'm so small," he sobbed,
"GRUESSES don't want to know."

"Exercises are the answer,
Each morning you must DO SOME."
He thanked me, smiled,

Pages 36–39

Many people prefer to write letters by hand rather than type them. They feel that it gives their letters a more considered and personal feel. These pages require children to follow fictional examples of letters written for public consumption. Some children may simply wish to complete the exercises as given. Others may wish to apply the idea to a problem in their own locality. They might make a comparison between this letter of complaint and examples found in their local newspaper. They may wish to design their own ideal leisure area within a local park or on a piece of waste ground. Groups of children might write to their local councillors, expressing the problem and suggesting some solutions. (It may be interesting to note whether handwritten letters receive handwritten replies!)

The remaining pages of Book 6 present activities designed to make children think about the different purposes of handwriting, and to practise their skills of neatness, layout and presentation.

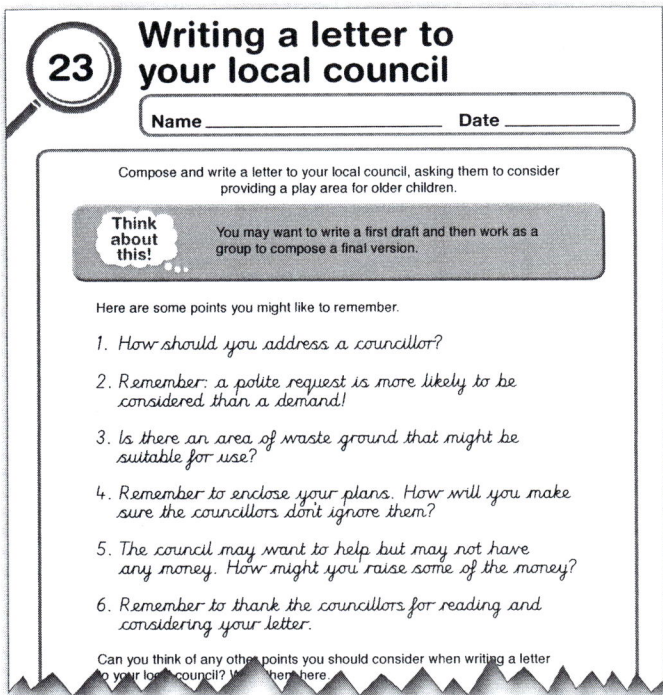

23 **Writing a letter to your local council**

Name _____ Date _____

Compose and write a letter to your local council, asking them to consider providing a play area for older children.

Think about this! You may want to write a first draft and then work as a group to compose a final version.

Here are some points you might like to remember.

1. How should you address a councillor?

2. Remember: a polite request is more likely to be considered than a demand!

3. Is there an area of waste ground that might be suitable for use?

4. Remember to enclose your plans. How will you make sure the councillors don't ignore them?

5. The council may want to help but may not have any money. How might you raise some of the money?

6. Remember to thank the councillors for reading and considering your letter.

Can you think of any other points you should consider when writing a letter to your local council? Write them here.

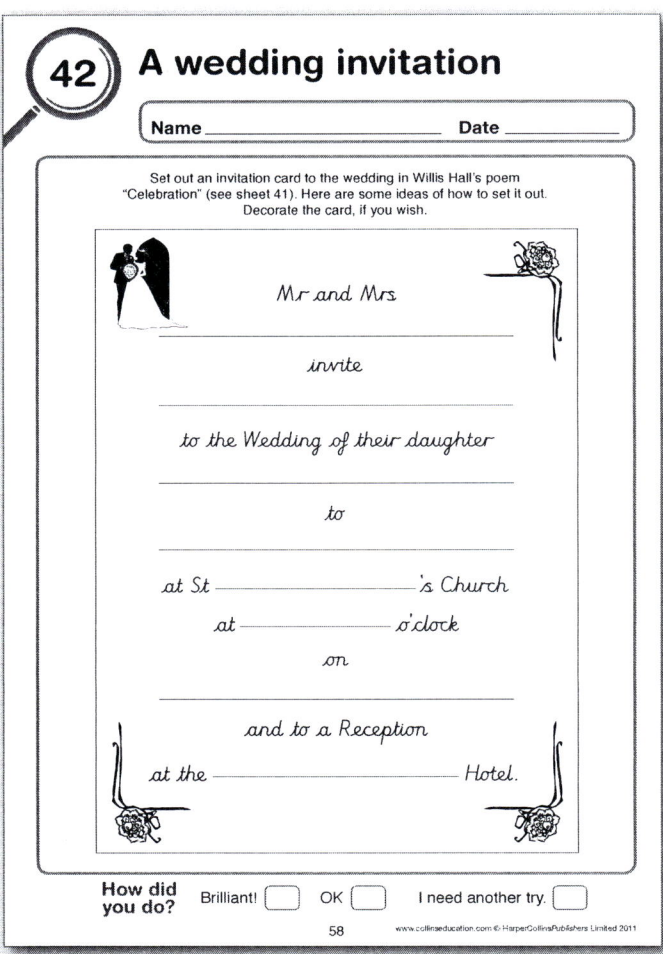

42 **A wedding invitation**

Name _____ Date _____

Set out an invitation card to the wedding in Willis Hall's poem "Celebration" (see sheet 41). Here are some ideas of how to set it out. Decorate the card, if you wish.

Mr and Mrs _____
invite _____
to the Wedding of their daughter _____
to _____
at St _____ *'s Church*
at _____ *o'clock*
on _____
and to a Reception
at the _____ *Hotel.*

How did you do? Brilliant! ☐ OK ☐ I need another try. ☐

58 www.collinseducation.com © HarperCollinsPublishers Limited 2011

Page 64

A set of guidelines is included for use when teachers wish children to repeat or practise specific task pages on separate sheets of paper. Teachers may copy the page and children may write directly onto the page, or use it as a guide by placing it underneath a sheet of plain paper.

Your Handwriting folder

Name _____ **Date** _____

Use your best handwriting to design a cover for your handwriting folder.
Make a Title box and add your name and the date started.
Then you may decorate the borders.

Think about this! Exercise books and files often look very similar. By covering your books and files and decorating the covers, you can personalise them and make them last longer.

Decorative patterns

Name _____ Date _____

Here are some patterns that you might use to decorate your work.
Try these first and then design some patterns of your own.

Name _____ **Date** _____

Some people like to write a label in all their books to make sure that people who borrow them, return them. Your label might include a logo of your intertwined initials.

From the library of

This book belongs to

_____

It was bought on

_____

_____

How did you do?   Brilliant! ☐   OK ☐   I need another try. ☐

My handwriting:
A checklist

Name _____ Date _____

Use this checklist to think about your handwriting.
You may discuss your answers with your partner, if you wish.

<u>Presentation</u>

Can other people read your handwriting?	Yes	No
Does your handwriting look neat?	Yes	No
Do all your titles and headings stand out clearly?	Yes	No
Does your handwriting slope ...		
to the left?	Yes	No
to the right?	Yes	No
all over the place?	Yes	No
Can you judge the space you will need for titles and headings?	Yes	No
Do you have a special pen that you prefer to write with?	Yes	No
Has your best handwriting improved since last year?	Yes	No

<u>Style</u>

Do most of your letters join?	Yes	No
If you don't put your name on your page, is your handwriting still recognisable as yours?	Yes	No
Do you have a distinctive signature?	Yes	No
Does your handwriting flow easily?	Yes	No
Do you have one style for notes and another for presentational writing?	Yes	No

<u>Sustained work</u>

Can you produce legible handwriting when writing quickly?	Yes	No
If you write a long piece of work, does your handwriting get worse towards the end?	Yes	No

What action do you think you need to take to improve your handwriting?

5 All about me!

Use the set of lines below to write as much as you can about yourself.
You might use the lines to make a rough draft, which you then copy
out neatly and store in your handwriting folder.

_____

_____

_____

_____

_____

_____

_____

_____

_____

_____

_____

_____

_____

_____

_____

_____

_____

_____

_____

How did you do?   Brilliant! ☐   OK ☐   I need another try. ☐

Name _____ Date _____

Here is the web page for the company that publishes this book.
Web page headings must be clear and catch the eye. Make sure to look at
other web sites to see how printed handwriting is used for effect.

Collins · *freedom to teach*

Login   Register   Account   Basket

Customer Service 0844 576 8126   Contact your rep   Help

Home   Primary   **Secondary**

Search [   ] **Go**

Contact Us | Trade | International | About Us

Offers | Quick order

Subjects
All Primary
Early Years
Literacy
Mathematics
Science
History
Geography
Atlases
Religious Education
PSHE
Art and Music
Modern Languages
Revision

Primary

[Select]

New website!

BigCat

Visit for details of our 2011 Children's Writing Competiton and lots lots more...

Collins Education publish teaching resources for the Foundation Stage, Key Stage 1 and Key Stage 2, to support the teaching of literacy, numeracy and a range of other Primary school subjects. These include the award-winning guided reading scheme Collins Big Cat and the bestselling Collins New Primary Maths series. Collins are now also selling Folens Primary resources, which include Early Years and Belair A World of Display.

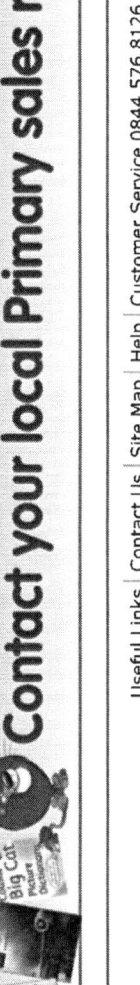

Contact your local Primary sales rep

Useful Links | Contact Us | Site Map | Help | Customer Service 0844 576 8126

7 Sign-writing

Name ______________________ Date ____________

Shop signs use many different letter styles in various shapes and sizes, as the examples below illustrate. Write what you think could be bought in each of these shops. On separate sheets of paper, design and colour three signs for shops. Make sure you use different letter styles and sizes for each sign. You can add decorative borders and motifs, if you wish.

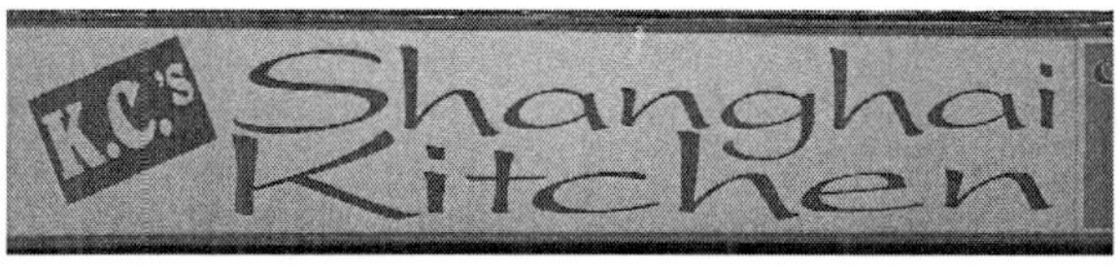

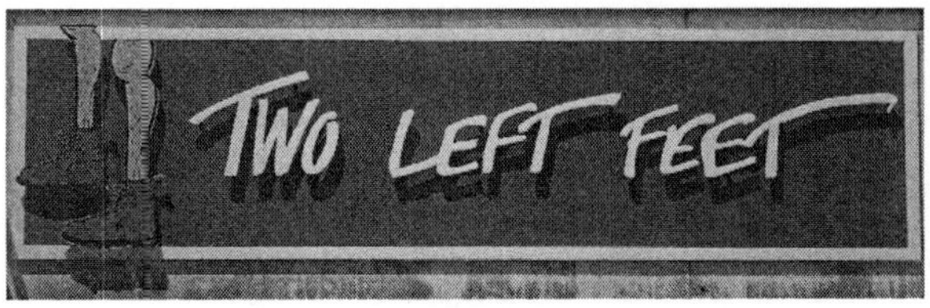

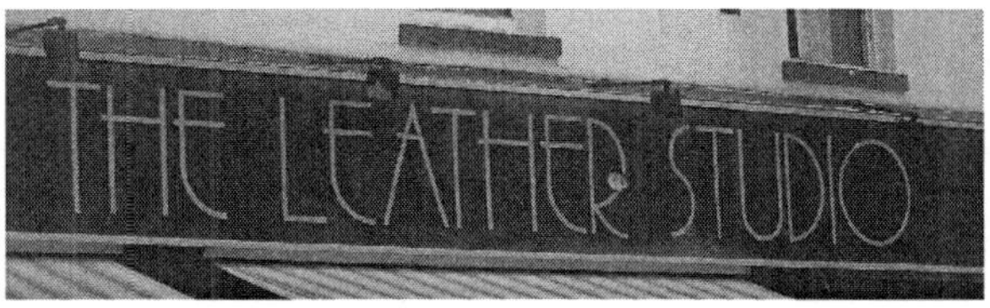

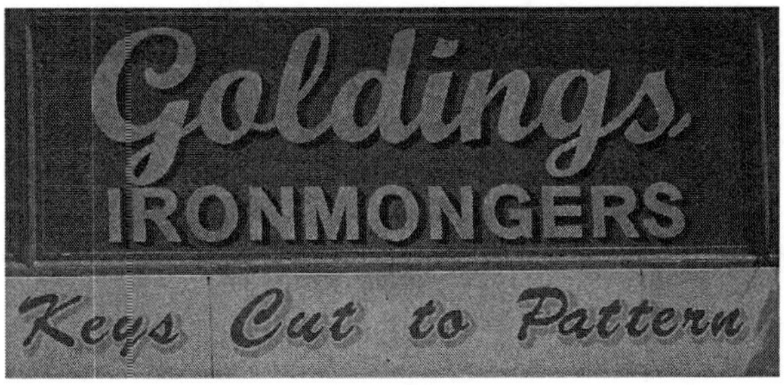

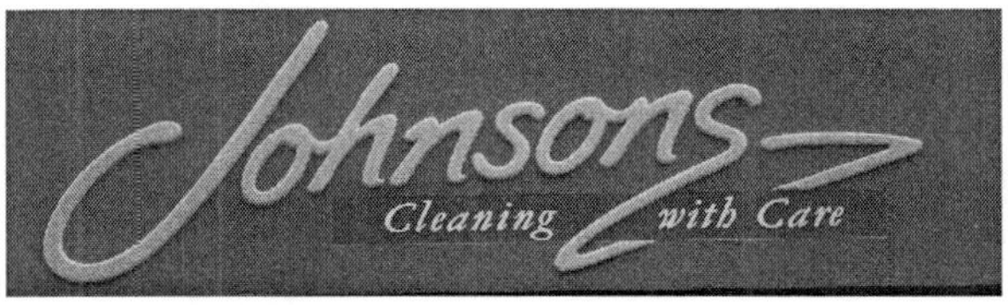

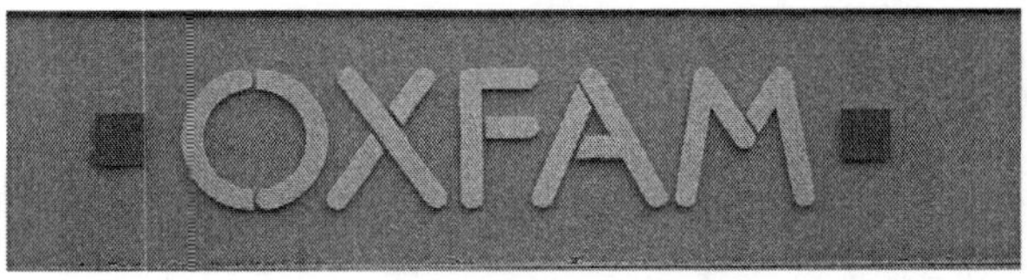

How did you do? Brilliant! ☐ OK ☐ I need another try. ☐

Designing labels

Name _____ Date _____

People use decorative lettering to label items in their garden.
Design some labels for the vegetables listed below, then decorate
the borders of each label.

Think about this!

Sometimes it is a good idea to first make a pencil draft
to check how long a label should be.

*Carrot   Parsnip   Cauliflower   Onion   Cabbage   Pea
Runner Bean   Potato*

How did you do?   Brilliant! ☐   OK ☐   I need another try. ☐

Decorating letters

Name _____ **Date** _____

Write and decorate the capital letters needed to complete
the days of the week.

onday

uesday

ednesday

hursday

riday

aturday

unday

How did you do? Brilliant! ☐ OK ☐ I need another try. ☐

Decorating letters

Write and decorate the capital letters needed to complete the names of the other eight planets in our solar system that orbit the Sun.

enus

upiter

atum

ercury

ranus

ars

luto

eptune

How did you do?   Brilliant! ☐   OK ☐   I need another try. ☐

Captions for photographs

Name _____ Date _____

Keeping special photographs in an album and labelling them helps you to remember when they were taken. Copy out the photo captions below.

Our kittens Pip, Bubble and Squeak: born 15th April 2000.

_____

_____

_____

A mother bear and her cubs: London Zoo, 20th July 2000.

_____

_____

_____

A very hairy Highland cow: Aviemore, 4th September 1999.

_____

_____

_____

Two swans flying away: Norfolk Broads, 3rd March 2000.

_____

_____

_____

How did you do?   Brilliant! ☐   OK ☐   I need another try. ☐

Name _____ Date _____

Copy part or all of this extract in your best handwriting.
You might use your Handwriting folder to store extracts from your
favourite stories or information books.

Think about this!

You may wish to **enlarge**, *italicise* or underline words
to enhance their impact.
Look at a range of texts to see how various other authors
use punctuation for effect.

Through the dark night a darker shape slid.
A sinister figure shrithed down from
the moors, over high shoulders, sopping tussocks,
over sheep-runs, over gurgling streams.
It shrithed towards the timbered hall, huge
and hairy slightly stooping. Its long arms
swung loosely ...
Through half-closed eyes Beowulf was
watching, and through barred teeth he
breathed one word. "Grendel." The name of
the monster, the loathsome syllables ...
Grendel saw the knot of sleeping men and
his eyes shone with an unearthly light.
He lurched towards the nearest man, a brave
Geat called Leofric, scooped him up and,
with one ghastly claw, choked the scream in
his throat. Then the monster ripped him
apart, bit into his body, drank the blood
from his veins, devoured huge pieces; within
one minute he had swallowed the whole
man, even his feet and hands.

How did you do?   Brilliant! ☐   OK ☐   I need another try. ☐

www.collinseducation.com © HarperCollins*Publishers* Limited 2011

Handwriting check 2:
"Gruesome"

Name _____ Date _____

Write this poem in your best handwriting and store it in your Handwriting folder. You might like to keep some more poems ready in case you need them.

I was sitting in the sitting room
toying with some toys
when from a door marked: "Gruesome"
There came a GRUESOME noise.

Cautiously I opened it
and there to my surprise
a little GRUE lay sitting
with tears in its eyes.

"Oh little GRUE please tell me
what is it ails you so?"
"Well I'm so small," he sobbed,
"GRUESSES don't want to know."

"Exercises are the answer,
Each morning you must DO SOME."
He thanked me, smiled,
and do you know what?
The very next day he ...

Roger McGough

How did you do?   Brilliant! ☐   OK ☐   I need another try. ☐

Name _____ **Date** _____

Design your own fiend as an illustration for a ghost story.
Label the different parts of your fiend to show what makes it really scary!
Remember to include the colours for the illustrator.

Hair like the (green) weeds in a garden.

Eyes

Teeth

Fingernails

Breath

Feet

How did you do? Brilliant! ☐ OK ☐ I need another try. ☐

Some words you should know

Name _____ **Date** _____

Write the words in the box in alphabetical order. Then practise reading and spelling them with your partner.

Think about this!

Practise writing each word several times.
You may want to write them in different styles to create a dramatic effect.

Frankenstein beast doppelganger vampire creature fiend ghost transmogrifier Dracula ghoul demon werewolf monstrosity

_____

_____

_____

_____

_____

_____

_____

_____

_____

_____

_____

_____

_____

_____

_____

How did you do?   Brilliant! ☐   OK ☐   I need another try. ☐

Some words you should know

16

Name _____ Date _____

Write the words in the box in alphabetical order. Then practise reading and spelling them with your partner.

Think about this!

Practise writing each word several times.
You may want to write them in different styles to create a dramatic effect.
When you have practised writing each word,
try to find an example of it and design a poster to show what the word means.

> obituary haiku epitaph rhyme tanka anecdote
> kenning saga ballad proverb limerick
> metaphor mnemonic

How did you do?   Brilliant! ☐   OK ☐   I need another try. ☐

www.collinseducation.com © HarperCollinsPublishers Limited 2011

Name _____ Date _____

Write this poem in your best handwriting. You might wish
to decorate it with scary images from the poem!

I don't believe in vampires,
I'll say it loud and clear,
I don't believe in werewolves,
When other folk are near.

I certainly don't believe in ghosts,
All those that do are fools,
And I know for an absolute positive fact,
There are no such things as ghouls.

So why, when it is late at night,
After all that I've just said,
Do vampires, werewolves, ghosts and ghouls
All gather underneath my bed?

The truth, of course, is obvious,
And plain for all to see,
For though I don't believe in them,
They all believe in me!

Willis Hall

Compiling a poetry anthology

Name _____ **Date** _____

As well as storing poems in your Handwriting folder, you may wish
to compile your own anthology of favourite poems.
Collect poems that match the categories below.

Think about this! When you are compiling your anthology, you will need
to use a colon, semi-colons or commas to separate titles.

Rhymes and Jingles

Playground Rhymes

Humorous Verse

Ballads, Sagas and Epic Poems

Sinister and Weird

Shape Poems

Limericks and Poetic Jokes

Beautiful, but Sad

Tanka

Haiku

Well-known Favourites

Romantic Verse

www.collinseducation.com © HarperCollins*Publishers* Limited 2011

19 A passage to punctuate:
"Street Child"

Name _____ Date _____

Write this extract, but make sure to insert the correct punctuation.

Think about this!

Think carefully about where commas might be placed in the extract. You might also wish to use dashes or brackets to emphasise meaning.

for most of the rest of the morning mr barrack read out loud to the boys pacing up and down as he did so the candle flames fluttered in his wake and his black shadow danced on the walls curled in his hand was the end of a knotted rope which he swung as he walked striking it across a desk from time to time to make the boys jump awake every now and then he stopped and pointed at a boy who had to stand up and recite the sentences hed just heard if he got it wrong mr barrack swung the knotted end of the rope across the boys hand

Berlie Doherty

_____
_____
_____
_____
_____
_____
_____
_____
_____
_____

How did you do?   Brilliant! ☐   OK ☐   I need another try. ☐

Writing a letter of complaint

Name _____ Date _____

Read through this letter of complaint and then write your own letter to a newspaper, complaining about something that annoys you.

To: The Editor

Dear Sir/Madam,

I am writing to complain about the behaviour of the young children and teenagers in my area. Yesterday, I went to visit an elderly neighbour who is terrified to go out of her house. She has been plagued by the children on her estate, putting rubbish through her letter box, calling names after her when she goes to the shop and now throwing stones at her windows.

Do the parents of these children know what they are up to? Are all children so rude and ill-mannered? My own children are now grown-up but I don't remember them getting into this sort of trouble! I understand that children want to be with their friends but do they need to hang around on street corners and harass the elderly? In my day, children were taught to be seen and not heard!

I hope that if you would be so kind as to print this letter in your newspaper, the parents concerned might take some action to stop this problem.

Yours faithfully,

Brenda Blenkinsop (Mrs)

Some points in reply

Name _____ Date _____

The Editor of the newspaper asked his own young son what he thought about the letter on sheet 20. Here are some of the points he made in reply. What points would you make? Set them out as bullet points, making sure to use the correct punctuation.

Dad,

There is no excuse for being rude and unkind to other people, but:

- The young people in this area have nowhere to go in the evenings;
- In summer we can go to the park, but this is no good in winter and our parents like us to stay near to the house;
- You can go to the pub for a drink but we have nowhere to meet;
- We like to talk privately but we can't do that in someone's house. Besides, no one has room for us;
- We do not mean to be threatening, but often when we laugh and joke, people think we are laughing at them;
- Old people can be just as rude as young people;
- Once we have done our homework, we want to do something interesting and have some fun;
- If we use our skates, skateboards or bikes, in the streets we get accused of knocking people down;
- The young children have an adventure playground but we are too old to use it;
- There used to be a Youth Club but it had to close through lack of funding.

I hope some of these points help to answer the lady's complaints. I must rush now because I want to finish my homework and go out with my mates!

Your ever loving son.

Designing a play area

Name _____ **Date** _____

The Editor's son made a plan of what he would like to see in a play area for older children. If you could design a play area, what would it contain? Here are some of the things you might want to include.

Think about this! How might you use arrows, dashes and brackets to make your meaning clear?

Seats (some with shelter from wet weather)

Mountain bike track with humps and hurdles

Rollerblade/ skateboard circuit

Football pitch/ basketball court

Cyber café (computers and soft drinks)

More seats

Garden

Writing a letter to your local council

Name _____ **Date** _____

Compose and write a letter to your local council, asking them to consider providing a play area for older children.

Think about this! You may want to write a first draft and then work as a group to compose a final version.

Here are some points you might like to remember.

1. How should you address a councillor?

2. Remember: a polite request is more likely to be considered than a demand!

3. Is there an area of waste ground that might be suitable for use?

4. Remember to enclose your plans. How will you make sure the councillors don't ignore them?

5. The council may want to help but may not have any money. How might you raise some of the money?

6. Remember to thank the councillors for reading and considering your letter.

Can you think of any other points you should consider when writing a letter to your local council? Write them here.

_____

_____

_____

_____

_____

_____

_____

24 Proverbs and sayings

Name _____ Date _____

Write these proverbs and sayings and then practise reading and spelling them with your partner.

Think about this! A proverb is a witty saying that tells a truth about the way we live.
Find a reference book of proverbs and copy out some of your favourites.

A bad workman always blames his tools.

_____

_____

_____

A drowning man will clutch at a straw.

_____

_____

_____

A friend in need is a friend indeed.

_____

_____

_____

A hungry man is an angry man.

_____

_____

_____

How did you do?   Brilliant! ☐   OK ☐   I need another try. ☐

25 Some words you should know

Name _____ **Date** _____

Write the words in the box in alphabetical order. Then practise reading and spelling them with your partner.

Think about this! Practise writing each word several times. You may want to write them in different styles to create dramatic effect.

autobiography glossary commentary hypothesis alliteration synopsis parody assonance narration biography appendix

_____

_____

_____

_____

_____

_____

_____

_____

_____

_____

_____

_____

_____

_____

_____

How did you do? Brilliant! ☐   OK ☐   I need another try. ☐

Name _____   Date _____

Write this extract, making sure you insert the correct punctuation.

the old ones stood in the doorway of the church their arms linked together none spoke a word to another wild noise and turbulence rose outside the light darkened the wind howled and whined the snow whirled in and whipped their faces with white chips of ice and suddenly the rooks were in the snow hundreds of them black flurries of malevolence cawing and croaking diving down at the porch in shrieking attack and then swooping up away

Susan Cooper

_____

_____

_____

_____

_____

_____

_____

_____

_____

_____

_____

_____

_____

How did you do?   Brilliant! ☐   OK ☐   I need another try. ☐

www.collinseducation.com © HarperCollins*Publishers* Limited 2011

Captions for cartoons

Name _____ **Date** _____

Draw some cartoons to illustrate these witty sayings.
Then write an informative caption beneath each image.

Don't throw the baby out with the bathwater.

_____

_____

_____

Take the bull by the horns.

_____

_____

_____

I'll believe that when pigs fly.

_____

_____

_____

The pen is mightier than the sword.

_____

_____

_____

How did you do?   Brilliant! ☐   OK ☐   I need another try. ☐

Designing labels

Name _____ Date _____

People often use decorative lettering to label plants in their garden.
Design some labels for the flowers listed below, then decorate
the borders of each label.

Rose Dahlia Rhododendron Daisy Daffodil Iris
Geranium Tulip Lily Chrysanthemum

How did you do?   Brilliant! ☐   OK ☐   I need another try. ☐

www.collinseducation.com © HarperCollins*Publishers* Limited 2011

Handwriting check 4:
"The Daffodils"

Name _____ Date _____

Write this poem in your best handwriting.

I wandered lonely as a cloud
That floats on high o'er vales and hills,
When all at once I saw a crowd,
A host of golden daffodils,
Beside the lake, beneath the trees
Fluttering and dancing in the breeze.

Continuous as the stars that shine
And twinkle on the Milky Way,
They stretched in never-ending line
Along the margin of the bay;
Ten thousand saw I at a glance
Tossing their heads in sprightly dance.

The waves beside them danced, but they
Outdid the sparkling waves in glee:
A poet could not but be gay
In such a jocund company!
I gazed - and gazed - but little thought
What wealth the show to me had brought.

For oft, when on my couch I lie
In vacant, or in pensive mood,
They flash upon that inward eye
Which is the bliss of solitude;
And then my heart with pleasure fills,
And dances with the daffodils.

William Wordsworth

Name _____ **Date** _____

Design an illustration for each of the following sayings and write
the relevant proverb underneath.

Great minds think alike.

*Two wrongs don't make
a right.*

*People in glass houses
shouldn't throw stones.*

_____
_____
_____

_____
_____
_____

_____
_____
_____

Think about this! These sayings are not intended to be taken literally.
They have a double meaning. We use them to make a point.
Think about how you might illustrate "There's many a slip
'twixt cup and lip!"

How did you do?   Brilliant! ▢   OK ▢   I need another try. ▢

Design an invitation

Name _____ **Date** _____

We all like to receive invitations to parties. If you were having a party,
what would you put on the invitations to be sent out? Use the example
below to help you design an invitation to your party.

You are invited to:

A Disco and Hot-pot Supper

with music by

The Pickled Onions

on

Tuesday 30th September

at 7:30pm

Please wear your best "bib and tucker".

32 My favourite party

Write a short description of your favourite party. The questions below might give you some ideas.

Would you have your party at home or somewhere else?

_____

Would you have your party in a different country?

_____

At what time of the year would it be held?

_____

Would you have it during the week or at the weekend?

_____

Would you choose a theme, e.g. fancy dress?

_____

How would you provide the music? Would a famous group play?

_____

What kind of food would you have?

_____

_____

Would you play party games?

_____

Would you invite lots of people or only a special few?

_____

How did you do?   Brilliant! ⬜   OK ⬜   I need another try. ⬜

Rules of behaviour for pupils

Name _____ **Date** _____

Write the rules listed below as a poster for display in your classroom.
Decide whether you think the rules should be written in print
or joined writing. You may decorate your poster, if you wish.

Rules of behaviour

1. Do not run in the corridors.
2. Do not talk during Assembly.
3. Do not chew gum in class.
4. Do not leave the classroom without permission from your teacher.
5. Do not drop litter in the playground.

Think about this!

Rules are called imperatives: they must be obeyed. Often they are there to ensure our safety.
Write a list of rules to help a young child cross a busy road.

Rules of behaviour for teachers

Name _____ **Date** _____

Did you know that rules also apply to teachers? In the nineteenth century, female teachers had to obey rules like the ones listed below. Write out some rules you would like your teachers to obey!

Think about this!

Remember: rules should be for safety or to keep order. You might like to discuss some suitable rules for your teachers with the rest of your group.

Rules of behaviour

1. You must be home between the hours of 8pm and 6am unless attending a school function.
2. You may not loiter downtown in the ice-cream stores.
3. You may not dress in bright colours.
4. You may under no circumstances dye your hair.
5. You must wear at least two petticoats.

_____

_____

_____

_____

_____

_____

_____

_____

_____

How did you do?   Brilliant! ☐   OK ☐   I need another try. ☐

Name _____ Date _____

Use this sheet to draft some rules of behaviour in your classroom.
You might then set them out as a poster.

_____
_____
_____
_____
_____
_____
_____
_____
_____
_____
_____
_____
_____
_____
_____
_____
_____
_____
_____
_____
_____
_____
_____
_____
_____

How did you do?   Brilliant! ☐   OK ☐   I need another try. ☐

Devising rules of behaviour

Name _____ **Date** _____

Use this sheet to draft some rules of behaviour for your teachers.
You might wish to illustrate your ideas.

_____
_____
_____
_____
_____
_____
_____
_____
_____
_____
_____
_____
_____
_____
_____
_____
_____
_____
_____
_____
_____
_____
_____
_____
_____
_____
_____

How did you do? Brilliant! ⬜ OK ⬜ I need another try. ⬜

Famous quotations
(Sir Winston Churchill)

Name _____ Date _____

Write part or all of each of these quotations in your
best handwriting. You might set them out as a poster for display.

"Many forms of government have been tried, and will be tried in this world of sin and woe. No one pretends that democracy is perfect or all-wise.
Indeed it has been said that democracy is the worst form of government except all those other forms that have been tried from time to time."

House of Commons, 11th November 1947

"I would say to the House, as I said to those who have joined this government, 'I have nothing to offer but blood, toil, tears and sweat.'"

House of Commons, 13th May 1943

"Never in the field of human conflict was so much owed by so many to so few."

20th August 1940

"To jaw-jaw is better than to war-war."

Washington DC, 26th June 1954

"This is the sort of English up with which I will not put."

Comment on people who went to great lengths to avoid using prepositions at the end of sentences

Think about this!
Now find some quotations from one of your favourite personalities, or a character in a book. Remember to refer to when and where the statements were made.

Some words you should know

Name _____ **Date** _____

Write these words in alphabetical order. Then practise reading
and spelling them with your partner.

legislative authority democratic bureaucrat politician
statutory political authoritative govern legal
legislation authorise statute democracy
bureaucracy government

_____

_____

_____

_____

_____

_____

_____

_____

_____

_____

_____

_____

_____

_____

_____

How did you do?   Brilliant! ☐   OK ☐   I need another try. ☐

Inventing words

Name _____ **Date** _____

Invent some words and write a definition for each of them.
Follow the style of the example below. Read the invented words to your
partner and ask them to guess what they mean.

"Dontopedology is the science of opening your mouth and putting your foot in it."

Prince Philip, the Duke of Edinburgh

_____

_____

_____

_____

_____

_____

_____

_____

_____

_____

How did you do?   Brilliant! ▢   OK ▢   I need another try. ▢

A speed writing test

Name _____ **Date** _____

Try to write, as quickly as you can, some rules for bike-riding and inline skating in the streets near your home.

Rules for bike-riding and inline skating

Think about this!

We often need to write very quickly. When we do so, it is often difficult to keep your best handwriting.
Did your letters still join?
Can your partner read what you have written?

How did you do?   Brilliant! ☐   OK ☐   I need another try. ☐

Handwriting check 5:
"Celebration"

Name _____ Date _____

Write this poem in your best handwriting.

Think about this! You might like to illustrate this poem, putting the speech into speech bubbles above the pictures. Remember to change the punctuation.

I don't like weddings, not at all,
I find them just a bore,
At least, that's how it's always seemed,
When I've been to them before,
There's all those boring relatives,
That come from far and near,
Scoffing little triangular sandwiches,
And swigging wine and pints of beer,
Saying, "Don't the bridesmaids all look sweet?"
and, "Isn't it a pity,
That the best man's wearing two old socks?"
or "Was ever a bride so pretty?"
But I can't wait for Saturday,
To see Aunt Beryl's face,
'Cos cousin Cheryl's marrying,
A Thing From Outer Space!

Willis Hall

A wedding invitation

Name _____ Date _____

Set out an invitation card to the wedding in Willis Hall's poem "Celebration" (see sheet 41). Here are some ideas of how to set it out. Decorate the card, if you wish.

Mr and Mrs

_____

invite

_____

to the Wedding of their daughter

_____

to

_____

at St _____ 's Church

at _____ o'clock

on

_____

and to a Reception

at the _____ Hotel.

How did you do?   Brilliant! ☐   OK ☐   I need another try. ☐

43

Proverbs and sayings

Name ______________________________ **Date** _______________

Write these proverbs and sayings and then practise reading and spelling them with your partner.

Marry in haste, repent at leisure.

____

____

____

____

Faint heart never won fair lady.

____

____

____

____

One man's meat is another man's poison.

____

____

____

____

Where there's a will, there's a way.

____

____

____

____

How did you do? Brilliant! ☐ OK ☐ I need another try. ☐

Name _____ Date _____

All of these sports teams exist, and each has an unusual name.
Create your own unusual team names in the empty boxes.

Hamilton Academicals

Grasshoppers Zurich

Glenbuck Cherrypickers

Minnesota Timberwolves

Harlequins

Sale Harriers

Ipswich Witches

Think about this!

Would you use print or joined writing to write a team name?
Think about the logo and strip of your favourite team.
Design a badge or T-shirt in the correct team colours.
Think about the meaning of some unusual team names.

How did you do? Brilliant! ☐ OK ☐ I need another try. ☐

www.collinseducation.com © HarperCollins*Publishers* Limited 2011

Famous quotations
(Sport)

Name _____ **Date** _____

Write some or all of these quotations in your best handwriting.
You might wish to illustrate your sheet with appropriate images.

"Boxing is glamourised violence."
Lord Taylor of Grufe

"There is one similarity between music and cricket.
There are slow movements in both."
Neville Cardus

"All you need to be a fisherman is patience and
a worm."
Herb Shriner

"Some people think football is a matter of life and
death ... I can assure you it is much more serious
than that."
Bill Shankly

"A horse is dangerous at both ends and uncomfortable in
the middle."
Ian Fleming

"You've got a goal. I've got a goal. Now all we need is a
football team."
Groucho Marx

"Golf is a game whose aim is to hit a very small ball
into an even smaller hole, with weapons singularly
ill-designed for the purpose."
Sir Winston Churchill

Writing a poem

Name _____ **Date** _____

Use the first verse of this poem to begin your own three-verse poem about picking teams for a sport of your choice. Write your two new verses on the lines below.

Picking Teams

When we pick teams in the playground,
Whatever the game might be,
There's always somebody left till last
And usually it's me.

I stand there looking hopeful
And tapping myself on the chest,
But the captains pick the others first,
Starting, of course, with the best.

Maybe if teams were sometimes picked
Starting with the worst,
Once in his life a boy like me
Could end up being first!

Allan Ahlberg

_____

_____

_____

_____

_____

_____

_____

_____

_____

_____

_____

_____

_____

Handwriting check 6:
"The Lady of Shalott"

Name _____ **Date** _____

Write this extract and assess how much your handwriting has improved
since you began your handwriting folder.

Willows whiten, aspens quiver,
Little breezes dusk and shiver
Thro' the wave that runs for ever
By the island in the river
              Flowing down to Camelot.
Four grey walls, and four grey towers,
Overlook a space of flowers,
And the silent isle imbowers
              The Lady of Shalott.

By the margin, willow-veil'd,
Slide the heavy barges trail'd
By slow horses; and unhail'd
The shallop flitteth silken-sail'd
              Skimming down to Camelot:
But who hath seen her wave her hand?
Or at the casement seen her stand?
Or is she known in all the land
              The Lady of Shalott?

Only reapers, reaping early
In among the bearded barley,
Hear a song that echoes cheerly
From the river winding clearly,
              Down to tower'd Camelot;
And by the moon the reaper weary,
Piling sheaves in uplands airy,
Listening, whispers "'Tis the fairy
              Lady of Shalott."

Alfred Lord Tennyson

How did you do? Brilliant! ☐ OK ☐ I need another try. ☐

oftware information

To install the pre-cursive and cursive fonts
used in this series in your school, please visit
www.kber.co.uk, and purchase a licence for
Handwriting for Windows Version 3.0.